THE
EASY YOGA
WORKBOOK

A COMPLETE YOGA CLASS IN A BOOK

THE
EASY YOGA
WORKBOOK

TARA FRASER

DUNCAN BAIRD PUBLISHERS

LONDON

The Easy Yoga Workbook
Tara Fraser

Distributed in the USA and Canada by
Sterling Publishing Co., Inc.
387 Park Avenue South
New York, NY 10016-8810

This edition first published in the UK and USA in 2010 by
Duncan Baird Publishers Ltd
Sixth Floor
Castle House
75–76 Wells Street
London W1T 3QH

Library of Congress Cataloging-in-Publication Data

Fraser, Tara.
  The easy yoga workbook : a complete yoga class in a book / Tara Fraser.
      p. cm.
  Includes bibliographical references and index.
  ISBN 978-1-84483-912-4
  1. Hatha yoga--Therapeutic use. I. Title.

  RA781.7.F724 2010
  613.7'046--dc22

                            2009032164

ISBN: 978-1-84483-912-4

10 9 8 7 6 5 4 3 2 1

Typeset in Helvetica Condensed and Trade Gothic Bold Condensed
Colour reproduction by Color & Print Gallery Sdn Bhd, Malaysia
Printed by Imago, Singapore

For information about custom editions, special sales, premium and corporate
purchases, please contact Sterling Special Sales Department at 800-805-5489
or specialsales@sterlingpub.com.

PUBLISHER'S NOTE
The information in this book is not intended as a substitute for professional
medical advice and treatment. If you are pregnant or are suffering from any
medical conditions or health problems, it is recommended that you consult a
medical professional before following any of the advice or practice suggested
in this book. Duncan Baird Publishers, or any other persons who have been
involved in working on this publication, cannot accept responsibility for any
injuries or damage incurred as a result of following the information, exercises
or therapeutic techniques contained in this book.

For Simon, a natural Karma Yogi.
I hope this might inspire you to become a Hatha Yogi too,
in your own good time! Thank you, with love.

Contents

SYMBOLS USED IN THIS BOOK

✓ Posture is good for ... / Solution to problem

✗ Avoid if ... / Problem with posture

❗ Take care if you suffer from ...

◎ See Chapter 3 for troubleshooting tips

Author's introduction

The process of learning Yoga has been described as being like peeling layers of skin off an onion, to discover the tiny heart at its centre. It is not that we are trying to learn something new through this practice, but simply to uncover something eternal, the Self, that has always been there but has become obscured with layers of learning and history.

I have kept this image in mind constantly while writing Easy Yoga and I hope it has helped me present the kind of daily yoga that I practise in the clearest and simplest form for the reader.

The point of a yoga practice is not to force yourself into painful contortions but to experience, observe and regulate the sensations that arise from the exercises, breathing and meditation. Inevitably, not everyone will find all parts of this book easy to do. We are all different and we all have our own unique combination of strengths and weaknesses. But I have tried to make all of the book easy to understand, easy to remember, and easy to get into. A starting point from which to develop.

Once you have begun your journey into yoga you can make your practice sessions as complicated as you like! Enjoy trying new things out for yourself, have the confidence to experiment – it really is very easy to start a basic practice.

The exercises in this book are the result of the work that I have done with my students, especially beginners, over the last few years. I thank them for being such willing and inspiring guineapigs and hope that this book will help launch a new generation of onion peelers into the world of yoga!

How to use this book

THIS BOOK contains all you need to begin a simple yoga practice at home with confidence. Please read pages 22–25 before you start to do yoga postures, they contain some basic safety guidelines and simple general instructions you will need to get started.

• Chapter 1 offers a little background information explaining the benefits and basic principles of yoga.

• Chapter 2 gives you a selection of postures.

• Chapter 3 suggests variations and modifications of these poses. Turn to this section if you are finding a pose in Chapter 2 too difficult or would like to try a variation. This chapter answers some of the questions most commonly asked in a beginner level yoga class.

• Chapter 4 explains yoga breathing and meditation. These techniques are easier and more effective if they are practised after a basic session of postures.

• Chapter 5 gives some extra guidance for people who wish to use yoga as an additional technique to improve a sport. Yoga is widely recognized as an ideal form of cross-training and this chapter will help you select an appropriate yoga practice to complement your other activities.

CHAPTER 1:
Easy Principles

Beginning yoga is easy! Whatever your age and physical condition you can embark on a yoga practice today and gain some instant benefits, such as a lift in your mood and energy level, a feeling of calmness and relaxation, and a better night's sleep. Over the longer term, yoga helps you maximize your health and fitness and reduce the symptoms of stress and tension that so many of us suffer in our daily lives. In this chapter, you will find simple explanations of why yoga works and what it can do for you. There are also clear examples of what makes yoga different from other forms of exercise and details of how to put a personal practice together that will suit you and your lifestyle.

What is yoga?

Yoga is a technique for leading a healthy and fulfilling life. Combining instructions for exercise, lifestyle and meditation, yoga offers us a practical, adaptable framework for living our daily lives in peace, good health and constant self-development. It nourishes the whole person – mind, body and soul.

The origins of yoga can be traced back to civilizations living in India more than 2,000 years ago. The word "yoga" has many meanings but is often translated as "union", reflecting yoga's emphasis on the connection between body, mind and emotions. In the West, we have been practising yoga for more than 100 years – it has become as important for many of us as it was for the ancients in India.

Yoga as a practice covers a wide variety of disciplines, all of which aim toward the realization of the Self, or ultimate unity. In much the same way as the term "games" could cover pastimes as different as football and chess, yoga encompasses all kinds of activity – from meditation and chanting to headstands.

This book concentrates on a type of yoga known as Hatha ("sun/moon" or "forceful") yoga, which focuses on postures and breathing exercises. In the West, this is the most widely known form of yoga. The exercises are based on traditional teachings with some adaptations to make them more suited to modern Western living. For example, some of the exercises originally called for the student to adopt Lotus position – a cross-legged pose similar to that used daily in traditional Indian society, but that does not always come naturally to us in the West. The point is that whichever position we choose should be comfortable and so we may have to adapt by using some padding or perhaps a chair – thereby following the spirit, rather than the letter, of the ancients. The exercises are very simple; they just require patient practice on the part of the student.

Breathing exercises (known as *pranayama*) are vitally important in yoga. The breath connects the mind and body, and so by learning close control of our breathing through yoga, we can begin to make a positive change in our mental and emotional patterns.

You will experience an instant positive effect from both the breathing exercises and the postures. Most people report a feeling of ease and a release of tension with a simple practice lasting just 20 minutes. Over time this sensation can deepen and eventually you will be able to feel the benefits of your yoga practice in all aspects of your life.

You do not need to hold any particular beliefs to do yoga, nor do you need any special equipment. While access to a good teacher is useful, yoga is essentially a process of self-observation, -development and -realization, so the most important thing is for you to practise yoga for yourself, by yourself, with confidence. This book aims to help you do just that.

Why is yoga different?

The rise in the popularity of yoga has had the positive effect of making yoga classes accessible for everyone. However, it may also have helped foster a misunderstanding about the nature of yoga, equating it with forms of exercise such as Pilates or aerobics. Yoga differs from these in that it is not concerned solely with the musculo-skeletal body. It operates on other levels, such as the deep tissue, the internal organs and the endocrine and nervous systems.

Yoga also has a theory of an "energetic" or esoteric anatomy – one that we cannot see but the effects of which we feel. The esoteric body has a form of energy passing through it called *prana* (loosely translated as "life-force").

Postures and breathing exercises allow us to manipulate *prana*, helping to keep our bodies strong and healthy. Most importantly, yoga's philosophy and its ability to affect our mental and emotional states enable it to become a tool for radical change and self-development.

Unlike other exercise systems, yoga has so many different aspects that there is no set way to experience it. Many people come to yoga for the same reason: because their bodies feel tight, uncomfortable or weak and they are experiencing symptoms of stress and tension induced by their hectic lifestyles. They perform a series of easy yoga postures and breathing exercises and soon begin to feel much better. Some people go on to seek an in-depth study of the meditative or philosophical aspects of yoga, whereas others continue to derive benefit from their initial simple exercises for many years, without any need to consider *prana* or the esoteric body.

The multiplicity of approaches to yoga is reflected in the multiplicity of types of yoga. The general term "Hatha yoga" encompasses all yoga that uses postures (see p.12). Some forms, such as Astanga yoga, Power yoga and Dynamic yoga, are strong and mainly physical. Others, such as Sivananda yoga, Viniyoga and Bihar yoga, integrate spiritual teaching with the breathing exercises and postures. The postures and breathing practices in this book are common to almost all these forms. You will find these exercises practised, perhaps with some variation, at any yoga class.

Although yoga offers benefits not to be found in other forms of exercise, it has been pointed out that it lacks the aerobic element needed to keep the heart and lungs really healthy. This is true to an extent, especially if your yoga practice is quite gentle. Activities such as walking or cycling can compensate for this deficiency, as well as giving you a good reason to take your eyes off the computer screen for once and get some fresh air – a restorative experience in itself. However, by combining yogic breathing techniques and fairly vigorously performed standing poses, you will achieve a gentle form of aerobic exercise.

Stiffness and stretching

Many people reject the very thought of yoga because they think they are too stiff. Yet these are the very people who would benefit most. Stiffness is endemic in our population – even the young suffer pain, discomfort and limited mobility through chronic tension and muscle stiffness. We may get a little stiffer as we get older, but we can still maintain a really good degree of flexibility throughout our lives simply by stretching our muscles regularly.

What makes us stiff? Our bodies tighten or brace in order to avoid or minimize the impact of pain. For example, if you break a bone, the nearby muscles stiffen to act like a natural splint. Or, think how the muscles tighten as you flinch when you are about to have an injection.

Muscles tense in readiness for combat or to flee danger (the "fight or flight" response). This natural mechanism, essential for survival, is also indiscriminate. It is activated not only when we are in physical danger, but also when we are under emotional pressure – perhaps as a result of a looming deadline, or a heated confrontation. Problems arise if we don't relax the response fully after the crisis has passed.

We can spend our whole lives in an unconscious and unnecessary state of tense alert. We may notice symptoms such as general fatigue (it is very tiring holding the body in perpetual readiness for action!), poor mobility, painfully stiff muscles, back pain, digestive problems, anxiety, headaches, and all the other facets of stress. Stiffness can occur in one or two isolated places (commonly the neck, shoulders, hips and low back) or all over the body. A stiff muscle is one that cannot fully relax any more. Muscular stiffness has a knock-on effect on breathing and on the circulation of body fluids. Stiff muscles are not fully nourished by the blood and lymph systems and do not rid themselves completely of waste products, becoming congested and dry.

Stretching helps the muscles to relax. It sends messages to the brain to tell it that the emergency has passed, and re-educates the body out of habitually held stress-induced postures reminding it of what a normal posture is like. It helps to re-balance and fine tune all body systems so that they respond even more effectively to an emergency when one arises but relax quickly and fully once it has passed.

The role of the mind is important, too, so absent-minded stretching is of little use. Yoga poses demand that we stay fully focused on what is happening in the body as we stretch into the posture. In this way we use the poses as an analytical method for understanding ourselves at a deep level, seeing the changes in the body, breath and mind as a posture progresses. You will not injure yourself doing yoga as a direct result of this careful inward attention. Without it you are likely to find that the body reverts to its habitual stress response patterns even while you are doing the postures.

Passive and active stretching

As you begin to do yoga poses you may notice that you have a "good" and a "bad" side – one side is more flexible than the other. Most of us are fairly symmetrical at birth but become asymmetrical as we start to move about. Being right- or left-handed means that we favour one side of the body for certain movements. If you usually carry a handbag on one shoulder, or cross one leg over the other when sitting, you reinforce this asymmetry throughout your life.

Yoga helps even out asymmetry to a great extent but won't eradicate it entirely, and this would not be necessary or desirable. If you are aware that your posture is asymmetrical you could practise asymmetrical postures, as these quickly help to restore balance. For example, you might repeat a pose three times – first on the "bad" side, then the "good" side and then on the "bad" side again.

You may also find it beneficial to work with deep relaxation and passively held stretches, in which you place the body in a posture and

passive stretching

active stretching

relax as fully as possible. This method helps to get down to a deeply held tension that has become re-enforced by habitual movement (such as a slight limp that you have retained years after the original injury has healed).

The postures pictured on these pages help to open up the hip sockets. On the right, there is active use of muscles in the torso and arms as they push down to help stretch the legs. On the left, gravity does the work as you recline in the posture and passively stretch while letting your whole body relax. Both methods are useful and we should practise a combination of the two to get the full benefit from stretching.

Muscles generally work in pairs, one set lengthen as the opposite set contract.

For example, when the biceps contracts the triceps stretches. Yoga poses counterpose one another so that every muscle is both stretched and contracted during a practice.

Stretching is essential to fitness and well-being because flexibility is necessary for ease. Training programmes that emphasize strength and endurance can cause mental and physical imbalance. Stretching is an interior process, not about reaching goals and pushing limits but about finding space and letting go of tension.

Yoga as an antidote to work

Our bodies are designed to be on the move constantly throughout the day, alternating standing, squatting and kneeling positions with stretching, twisting, reaching and lifting poses, as well as walking, running and being still. The eyes, too, are made for high activity, switching rapidly from close, detailed focus to broad horizons, and back. However, for most of us the reality is that we spend at least some hours a day hunched over a desk or computer, crammed into a driving seat, slumped in front of the television or operating machinery.

It is hardly surprising that back pain is a universal complaint in industrialized nations. If we lack strength in the muscles that support the skeleton, we will develop areas of chronic tension and stiffness and begin to loose awareness of our bodies as we get utterly absorbed by the computer, TV, or task in hand.

Obviously, the very best way to rid yourself of the stresses and strains of modern life is to opt out of it and change your job for something more physically active and stress free. A few people actually carry this through, but for most of us it is a question of trying to cope better with our given circumstances. Yoga helps you to counter the negative mental and physical effects of prolonged periods of inactivity and poor posture. It is a way of re-awakening the body to its full potential. You will be asking your body to stand, squat, kneel, lie, twist and bend in all directions. You will extend and compress every inch of your body thoroughly and systematically, allowing the muscles to soften and strengthen and the mind to remember what it is to be aware of the body!

Yoga is not the only way of countering the effects of a modern working lifestyle, but I believe it is one of the best. The scope of yoga postures is huge, more comprehensive and more balanced (working equally on upper body and lower body, back and front, internal and external muscle) than most sports or aerobic-style workouts. A good example of this is the various ways yoga works on the hands and feet. Think how important it is to exercise the hands and feet properly if you spend your week wearing cramped shoes and typing at a PC.

Yoga treats the whole of you as one interconnected mechanism and therefore prescribes exercises for your eyes, your mental focus, your breathing systems, and your emotional state as well as your muscles and digestive system. Perhaps most important, the basic principles of yoga are easy to grasp and so a simple practice can be started by absolutely anyone who wants to try.

For those who want to take the plunge, yoga also provides an almost bottomless resource of personal development and exploration far beyond the confines of muscles and joints. This means that you can continue to practise yoga for the rest of your life and yet never get it perfect – and never get bored!

Creating an easy practice

When planning your yoga practice you should take into account all aspects of your life and surroundings. For example, those with small children may have little time alone to practise. In that case let them join in! A few minutes of postures are fun and beneficial for all of you.

If you are able to practise on your own for an hour or more each day that is wonderful. If not, don't despair. Just 10 minutes a day is worthwhile and a longer session occasionally will feel like a luxury!

In cold weather, you may need to do lots of strong work to warm up. When it's hot you may prefer to practise breathing exercises and meditation until the temperature cools, or reserve yoga for the coolest part of the day.

If you prefer morning sessions, you will need to do strong standing poses to get you going. You will feel much stiffer in the morning than in the evening. If you practise last thing at night, aim to make it calming and quietening to prepare the body for sleep. If you do vigorous standing poses, make sure you counter with gentle forward bends and passive postures such as Tailor pose (see p.64). Otherwise, keep to gentle postures so that you end your practice feeling calm and refreshed.

SELECTING POSTURES: Generally speaking, a complete practice should contain a mixture of postures with a range of spinal movements such as forward and backward bends, side bends and twists, plus standing, lying, inverted and sitting poses. But from time to time it is possible to plan a practice that focuses on just one aspect, such as lying down postures, that will be highly beneficial as well.

You need to be aware of how the postures make you feel during a practice and afterward. Once you begin to notice this you can quickly adapt a sequences of postures to suit you.

Think about what the yoga practice is for. If you are an athlete recovering from an injury, yoga offers gentle therapeutic rehabilitation. If you have a desk job and feel overweight and sluggish, you might prefer a vigorous yoga practice to counterbalance your work life. In all cases, take it slowly, work up to things bit by bit and never overdo it. Yoga should not hurt while you are doing it – nor the next day!

OTHER CONSIDERATIONS: Seek the advice of a qualified teacher if you are pregnant, injured, unwell, elderly or have restricted mobility. The traditional advice in yoga is not to do a strong practice while you have your period and to avoid all inverted postures (Shoulder stand, Headstand, Bridge and Dog).

Although there is little Western medical evidence to support this belief, it seems fair enough to let nature take its course and not turn the body upside down, causing blood to flow back into the body. Most women prefer to do a softer practice at this time, anyway.

Practical basics

The questions asked most frequently about yoga practice are: how much and how often? The answer is that it depends entirely on you.

Someone who works long hours in a demanding job may feel stressed and tense much of the time and exhausted at weekends. On their days off they may have enough time and energy only to do the chores.

A person with this sort of lifestyle could start with a 15-minute practice on alternate evenings or mornings as a way of unwinding or preparing for the day. This might build into a short daily practice, bringing restfulness and clarity to cope with their demanding schedule.

Alternatively, suppose someone had a very low-pressure life, with an undemanding or monotonous job. Perhaps they feel lethargic and unmotivated much of the time. They might wish to inject a little energy into their life and so would benefit from a regular morning practice of strong yoga postures and breathing exercises lasting 40 to 60 minutes in total.

You will soon get a feel for what suits you best and how to adapt a practice for yourself. Ten minutes of yoga once a week is better than no yoga at all. Generally speaking, it is better to do a short practice every day than a long one once in a while, but if that is how your time works out, take the opportunity to do your yoga! If you are routinely doing more than an hour a day you should perhaps get in contact with a qualified teacher to help guide you.

DO'S AND DON'TS: Here are some tips to ensure your session is both enjoyable and beneficial:

•Do wear loose clothing and go bare foot.

•Do practise in a warm, well-ventilated room.

•Do use a small cushion and a yoga block. If you don't have a yoga block, use a large book (such as a telephone directory). A non-slip yoga mat is useful, too, but not essential.

•Do breathe through your nose on both inhale and exhale. Every breath you take should be smooth, soft and steady: check it constantly.

•Do use a chair for some postures. Ideally, one with a hard seat and an open back. Make sure that it won't slip. You might need it for meditation and breathing exercises, too, if you can't sit comfortably on the floor.

•Don't practise in the mid-day sun.

•Don't practise on a full stomach – leave at least a 90-minute gap after a meal. The best time is early morning, before breakfast.

•Don't drink water while you are practising the postures. Wait until after you have finished.

•Don't strain in any of the poses or breathing exercises, and if any posture hurts come out of it slowly and carefully.

•Don't habitually practise in front of a mirror as this makes you concentrate on what the pose looks like and not how it feels.

•Don't worry if you don't look exactly like the pictures – your body is unique. Follow the instructions carefully, step by step, and feel your way to your best expression of the pose.

CHAPTER 2:
Easy Postures

Here are 22 basic poses to choose from as the basis of your yoga practice. They have been selected because they are simple, classic poses that involve a broad range of movements and work the whole body. For each one, you will find a photograph of the posture you are aiming for, as well as instructions that tell you how to get in to and out of the pose, and how to maintain it. Some poses are more challenging than others, some require more strength, and some require more flexibility. If you find yourself struggling with any pose, have a look in Chapter 3 to find out how you can modify the pose to make it easier.

Standing and balancing

GOOD FOR:
balance; coordination;
feeling centred

STANDING Stand with your feet a few inches apart and parallel. Lengthen your legs. Gently draw up your low-abdominal muscles and relax your shoulders and buttocks. Let your chin dip slightly to lengthen the back of your neck. With your arms relaxed at your sides, gently stretch your fingers downward. Breathe smoothly and evenly.

BALANCING Focus straight ahead. Breathing in, simultaneously raise your arms overhead and your heels off the floor to come to a balance. Breathing out, lower your heels and arms to come back to standing.

NOTES

Stand perfectly still, feeling your body balanced and strong with minimum muscular effort. Find the point at which your weight is centred over your feet, so that there is equal pressure on the balls of your feet and your heels and on your left and right legs.

For the balance, lift your arms up to your sides (this is a little easier) or in front of you. Choose one or the other or alternate on each breath. The aim is to coordinate the breath, the big arm movement and the tiny heel lift so that they all begin and end together.

This exercise provides the sense of grounding, stability and centredness you need to begin a yoga practice. Don't rush through it to get on to something more exciting – take your time to get it right. It is not as easy as it may seem!

Forward bend

✔ GOOD FOR:
hamstrings; digestion;
spinal flexibility

❗ TAKE CARE IF
you suffer from: acute
back pain; sciatic pain

◎ SEE PP.74–5

From a standing position with your feet a few inches apart, inhale and lift your arms over your head. As you exhale, fold forward from the hips, keeping your back long. Move your arms down your sides as you go, bring your hands or fingers to the floor. Bend your knees if necessary to release your low back. Relax your neck, jaw and upper back, then inhale and swing your body back up, now circling the arms up your sides to the overhead position. Repeat 6 times slowly and carefully, or hold for a few breaths for a more intense practice.

NOTES

The aim is not to "touch your toes" but to achieve a soft and relaxed forward bend that is coordinated with your breath. It will feel a little easier with each repetition.

Forward bends like this help to stretch the back and the backs of the legs. They also stimulate the digestive and eliminative systems and are a good way to warm up the body gently. Bringing the head down low helps to reduce upper back and neck tension.

Forward bends in general have an introspective feel to them and can help you to concentrate and tune in your awareness, especially at the beginning of a practice. They may help you to see things from a new perspective or to clear your head if you feel stressed.

Warrior

GOOD FOR:
thighs; abdominal strength and stamina; lack of confidence; mild depression

TAKE CARE IF you suffer from: very high blood pressure; acute low-back pain

SEE PP.76–7

Start with your feet together. Turn out your right foot a little and take a long step forward with your left foot, keeping it parallel. Try to keep your hips facing forward. Breathe in and lift your arms overhead, breathe out and bend into your front knee, lunging as far as you can without lifting your back heel. Inhale and stretch your arms strongly upward. Look up a little, keeping your neck long and throat relaxed. Try to lift your abdominal muscles. Stay for 2 to 6 breaths, then release your arms and step your feet back together. Repeat on the other side.

NOTES

This is an invigorating posture that makes your legs work hard and stretches your spine deeply. Although it is a strong pose, be careful not to practise it so strongly that it becomes a strain. Use your breathing to help you to keep a little movement in the pose when you are pressing firmly down with the outer edge of your back heel and lifting your belly muscles at the same time (the lifting of the abdominals helps support your back).

This pose can make you feel pleasantly alert and helps to build stamina and strength. It is good for helping you to confront challenges in your life with confidence and steadfastness.

Side lunge

GOOD FOR:
hips and thighs; abdominal strength; aiding awareness

TAKE CARE IF
you have an existing knee injury or groin strain

SEE P.78

Set your feet wide apart. Turn out your left foot and turn in the toes of your right foot a little. Inhale and lift your arms to shoulder height, stretching both legs and lengthening your torso. As you exhale, bend your left knee into a deep lunge, keeping it directly above your toes. On your next out-breath, lower your left forearm onto your thigh, then breathe in and lift your right arm overhead to form a clear diagonal line from heel to finger tips. Keep your back leg straight. Stay for 2 to 6 breaths, then repeat on the other side.

NOTES

This posture increases hip flexibility, stamina and strength. It tones the whole torso and the internal organs and helps to develop good abdominal support for the spine. You will feel an opening effect along the side of your body, particularly in the hip socket and the groin. Try to put lots of energy through the diagonal line that your body creates in the pose so that it feels uplifting and energizing – rather than slumping your weight gratefully onto your elbow and thigh! Your shoulders should be relaxed and soft, not hunched up round your ears. Don't clench your teeth! There is an element of endurance in this pose, which makes it good practice for the weak-willed or those who have lost their enthusiasm for life.

Triangle

GOOD FOR:
strength and flexibility in hips, ribs and legs

TAKE CARE IF you have existing low-back pain or a knee injury

SEE P.79

With your feet far apart, turn out your left foot and turn in the toes of the right a little. Lift your arms to shoulder height as you inhale. Pull up your leg muscles strongly and roll your left thigh back so your knee is directly above your ankle. As you exhale, make a deep fold at your left hip, extend the torso and put your left hand on your shin. Lift your right arm overhead and roll the right side of your torso open into a flat sideways bend. Look to your right thumb. Stay for 2 to 6 breaths, then inhale to come up to standing. Now repeat on the other side.

NOTES

This is a strong stretch that opens the sides of the body, expanding the ribs and increasing breathing capacity. It also works the hip sockets while strengthening and realigning the legs. You need to support your spine with your low-abdominal muscles, otherwise you will feel very heavy in the pose. The idea is that your arms extend like eagle wings from the back, rather than that you prop your body weight up on your left arm! Try to make yourself feel as if you are gliding in the pose.

To get it right, the pose requires strength and concentration. Focus your mind completely on your body, and make sure that you do not transfer the effort of the pose into strain in your neck or face. Unclench your teeth!

Standing twist

GOOD FOR:
mild low-back pain; digestion; spinal flexibility; diabetes; insomnia

TAKE CARE IF you suffer from: sciatic pain; acute back pain

SEE PP.80–81

Stand with your feet wide apart and parallel to each other. Draw up the muscles in your knees and thighs and feel your feet firm and square on the floor. On an in-breath, lift your arms to shoulder height and then as you exhale bring your right arm across to your left ankle or shin. Keeping your low-abdominal muscle drawn in to help support your spine, stretch your left arm upward. Bring your chest as close to your thigh as you can. Take 1 or 2 breaths in the pose and then repeat on the other side. Do the pose 2 to 4 times on each side.

NOTES

This pose combines strong work for the legs with a deep twisting and forward-bending action for the torso. It massages the internal organs, particularly the kidneys and digestive system. It extends and twists the spine and stretches the backs of the legs.

If you breathe deeply in the pose, you can develop the twisting action a little further with every exhalation and lengthen the spine with every inhalation.

Standing twists can be refreshing and open new perspectives if you are feeling jaded or that you are stuck in a rut. Turning your torso to face the opposite way from your legs may seem like a challenge if your attitude tends toward narrowness or inflexibility. Twists can help to unblock the mind and aid decision-making.

Mighty pose

GOOD FOR:
upper back weakness
or tension; weak legs

TAKE CARE IF
you suffer from: acute
knee problems; very
high blood pressure

SEE P.82

Stand with your feet a few inches apart and parallel. Raise your arms overhead on an in-breath. As you exhale, push your hips back and bend your knees into a deep squat. Ensure your knees track straight forward over your toes and don't collapse inward or bow outward. As you complete the movement and the out-breath, let your arms drop to the floor and your head and neck relax completely. Then inhale and stretch the whole spine, lifting your arms overhead and lengthening your legs to return to standing. Repeat 4 to 6 times.

NOTES

The challenge here is to keep your breath even and soft while doing what is quite a hard movement. Take particular care on the inhalation phase as you come back up from the squat. It needs to be a smooth, seamless move and it is essential to try to lift the arms and upper back first, which is much harder than just straightening your legs. If you can achieve this, you will dramatically strengthen your upper back. It is great for relieving the hunched-over feeling we acquire from spending hours at a desk or computer. The pose also builds stamina and strength in the legs and lengthens the Achilles tendon at the ankle, which makes it useful for people who run or play sports – and those who wear high-heeled shoes every day!

Dancer

GOOD FOR:
balance; sports
involving a lot
of running

TAKE CARE IF
you suffer from:
a knee injury; acute
low-back pain

SEE P.83

Stand with feet close together and parallel. Focus straight ahead of you and shift your weight onto the left foot. Lift your right foot and catch it with your right hand. Bring the right knee down low until it is as close as possible to the left. Relax your right thigh, and let the hip socket feel open, then lift your left arm overhead as you inhale. Still keeping a steady gaze, carefully move your foot back as far as you can without strain. Keep your belly muscles drawn up and tailbone lengthening down. Balance like this for 3 to 6 breaths. Repeat on the other side.

NOTES

The temptation to move your raised leg out to the side a bit in order to make it lift higher is great, but try to keep it totally parallel with your standing leg throughout. This way you get a deep stretch over the whole front of the thigh and a gentle, well-supported back bend. Try to focus your gaze on a point at eye level or a little higher, as this will encourage your chest to open and your breath to be full and deep. Your supporting leg should be completely straight and well drawn-up throughout, but think of the supporting foot being soft and wide as it touches the ground. There should be a joyous, uplifting feel about this pose, named after Nataraja – the lord of the dance in Hindu mythology. Don't let it become too tense and military!

Cat

GOOD FOR:
bad desk posture; upper back and neck tension

AVOID IF
you suffer from: acute knee problems

SEE P.84

Kneel on all fours, with your hands shoulder-width apart and your knees a little closer. As you inhale, bend your elbows and press your chest gently forward while rolling your shoulders back and down toward your waist. Turn your face and eyes up slightly at the end of the in-breath, then exhale to round your back in the other direction, drawing your head and tailbone toward each other and tucking your belly into your spine. Repeat 4 to 8 times, carefully synchronizing the movement with your breath, which should remain fluid throughout.

NOTES

This simple little pose can have an almost miraculous effect on the spine. It is a wonderful tonic for all the spinal nerves and tissues, and it helps to calm the mind, centre the body and senses, and free any pent-up tensions and anxieties you may have.

Above all, it is such a gentle and "easy" pose that most people will be able to manage it without difficulty.

It is absolutely essential to include this pose in your practice if you regularly spend hours sitting at a desk or in front of a computer. It will help to unknot your shoulders and release tension from your spine while providing a little gentle work for your abdominal muscles and arms. Take care not to do all the movement with your chin! The whole spine should move, not just your neck.

Dog

✓ GOOD FOR:
almost everything!

❗ TAKE CARE IF
you suffer from:
shoulder problems;
tennis elbow

✖ AVOID IF
you suffer from:
acute wrist problems
such as RSI; very high
blood pressure

◎ SEE PP.86–7

Kneel on all fours, with hands shoulder-width apart, fingers splayed and pointing forward, and knees hip-width apart. As you exhale, tuck your toes under you, raise your hips and straighten your legs. Keep your shoulders wide and let your head relax. Press your chest toward your ankles. Gently draw the lowest belly muscles into your spine. Tilt your pelvis up as far as you can. If your legs will straighten, pull up your thigh muscles and sink your heels into the floor. Stay for 1 to 6 breaths, then kneel and sit on your heels to rest. Repeat 3 to 6 times.

NOTES

This pose can completely transform your body in terms of strength, stamina, muscle tone and physical awareness. One of the key features of the pose is that it is somewhat "inverted", in that your head is lower than your hips. This helps to refresh the mind. While it can seem very challenging to begin with, even for people who are fit and strong, it soon becomes a position in which you can almost "rest". You need to make sure that you prioritize the lengthening and straightening of your spine over the stretching of your legs. Your hips must make a firm upward tilt in order to become fully at ease in the pose. Then your shoulders can be wide and relaxed. Close your eyes and breathe deeply and slowly, expanding your chest to the full.

Child

✓ GOOD FOR:
stress; anxiety;
insomnia; constipation

✗ AVOID IF
you suffer from:
a knee injury (use
knees-to-chest pose
as an alternative).

◎ SEE P.85

Kneel on the floor with your knees close together. Fold yourself gently forward until your head rests on the floor. Sweep your arms along beside your heels and let them relax on the floor. Feel the deep fold in your hips, knees and ankles, and become aware of the breath moving in you as your torso rests on your thighs. Relax the muscles in your face and jaw. Let your neck soften and relax your tongue in your mouth. Stay in the pose for as long as you feel comfortable, breathing easily and gently.

NOTES

It is really important that you feel comfortable in this pose. If it seems like hard work, then look at Chapter 3 for ways of modifying it to suit you. Once you are comfortable and can fully relax, this posture has a lovely pacifying effect and is excellent for people who feel stress or anxiety overwhelming them. The weight of the head and the weight of the pelvis drop downward with gravity to gently stretch the spine in both directions. Child pose allows you to drain all strain and tension out of your head into the ground. It leaves you feeling refreshed and relaxed; it gently massages the internal organs and develops flexibility in the knees, hips and ankles.

Shoulder stretch

GOOD FOR:
upper back and
shoulder tension;
breast health

TAKE CARE IF
you suffer from:
shoulder problems;
tennis elbow

SEE P.88

Kneeling comfortably, inhale and lift your right arm overhead. Bend your elbow, bringing your hand, palm facing down, onto your back. Take your left hand behind your back and, keeping its palm facing outward, try to grasp your right fingertips. On your next exhalation, lengthen the muscles in your low back and slightly "tone" your belly to create a strong, well-lifted torso with your back as straight as possible. Close your eyes, keep your head level and breathe evenly and fully for 3 to 8 breaths. Then repeat on the other side.

NOTES

This pose strongly stretches the shoulder area and helps to make us aware of the way limb movement can affect the alignment of the torso. It also involves a deep stretch across the front of the chest, which opens the body to new perspectives. It is quite normal to find the pose much harder to do on one side than on the other, as none of us is completely symmetrical. Most people find it harder to have their dominant arm in the lower position, because not only is it the stronger arm but it is also the stiffer.

In any pose where the hands meet and touch there is an element of "binding" – that is to say that we will feel a sense of energy flowing from one hand to the other, forming a loop of energy in the body. This sensation can be very reassuring and stabilizing.

Cobra

GOOD FOR:
upper back and shoulder tension; breath awareness

SEE P.89

Lie on your front with your arms bent and palms on the floor. Your hands should be quite far back, level with your ribcage. Balance your forehead on the floor and feel the back of your neck lengthen. As you inhale, lift your head and chest a little way off the floor, drawing your elbows slightly back and toward each other as you go. Allow your breath to open your chest gently. As you exhale, lower your head back down to the floor. Do the pose 4 to 8 times, slowly and carefully.

NOTES

This pose is an ideal antidote to daily work at a desk, especially if you spend a lot of time using a computer. The pose helps to strengthen and give increased flexibility to the upper back and shoulders. It also makes you very aware of the movement of breath in your body. The point here is to try to get the upper part of your back to lift and lengthen. Your arms do very little work and you may find that you can hardly lift your head clear of the floor. It's more important to stretch your body out lengthways than to arch backward a long way. Double check that you are not clamping your jaw shut as you do the pose. Above all, keep your breath smooth and even. Cobra pose should be a perfect balance of strength and softness.

Knees to chest

GOOD FOR:
shoulder, neck and upper back tension; back pain of all sorts; digestive problems; stress; anxiety

SEE P.90

Lie on your back drawing your knees toward your chest. Place one hand on each knee with the fingertips facing your feet. On each inhalation, allow your knees to move gently away from your body until your arms are roughly straight. As you exhale, fold your knees back in toward your chest very gently and effortlessly. Make sure your shoulders and upper body and neck remain relaxed throughout. Repeat as many times as you like (you can never do it too much!), but 5 or 6 rounds will probably be enough to have a positive effect.

NOTES

This is one of the most simple and most important restorative poses in the yoga repertoire. It lengthens the spine, massages the internal organs and creates a deep sense of harmony and relaxation. It is a wonderful exercise for people with persistent stress-related low-back pain. You need to do it really slowly and gently – probably at half the speed that you initially want to. Bear in mind that your knees only have to move a tiny fraction toward your chest – the key thing is to focus on your breathing and sense a folding in the hip on the out-breath and a slight release on the in-breath. You may notice a little pause between your inhalation and exhalation. Let it be there, and just wait for the next breath before you begin to move again. Take your time.

Leg lifts

GOOD FOR: strengthening the back and abdominal muscles; digestion; constipation; bladder problems

AVOID IF you suffer from: acute low-back pain

SEE P.91

Lie on your back with your knees drawn in to your chest and your arms by your sides. On an inhalation, simultaneously lift your arms overhead and stretch your legs upward. Keep your pelvis in contact with the floor and your legs vertical – avoid drawing them toward your head, if possible. Keep the back of your neck long and relaxed, with your chin drawn slightly toward your throat. As you exhale, lower your knees back into your chest while bringing your arms back down by your sides. Repeat 4 to 6 times, slowly and carefully.

NOTES

This is another one of those yoga exercises that, at first, does not seem to require much thought, but that yields its greatest benefits only to those who practise it with care and attention. Mechanical, unthinking repetition of the movement does not give the same effect. Take your time and really integrate the movement and the breath. Feel the back of the pelvis and sacrum (lower-back bones) on the floor and the way your muscles move as you change your leg position. In this way you will develop a deeper awareness of how the muscles of the back and abdomen operate. Try to do the whole posture very gently, without force, just finding a nice fluid style for the movement and the breath.

Boat

GOOD FOR:
weak abdominals;
poor posture

TAKE CARE IF
you suffer from: very
high blood pressure;
acute back pain

SEE P.92

Sit up straight with your knees bent and feet flat on the floor in front of you. Bring your knees and ankles together so that they are touching and link your hands underneath your knees. Lean back until your feet leave the floor, lifting them to knee height. As you do this, press the centre of your chest forward and strongly lift the whole spine using your abdominal muscles. When you feel steady, stretch your arms out in front of you, level with your knees. Take 3 to 6 even breaths in the pose, then lower your legs gently to the floor. Repeat 2 to 4 times.

NOTES

In boat pose you should be sitting up on your "sitting bones" not collapsing back onto your sacrum, or your coccyx – or tailbone. (You will be able to tell whether you are resting on your sacrum or coccyx because your back will then be rounded and the pose will feel very uncomfortable.) Try to really elevate your chest and make your belly muscles help to support your spine.

The pose quickly gets easier with a bit of practice. It is excellent for improving abdominal and spinal strength and stamina. It may help you to keep the pose soft and fluid and to avoid straining if you picture yourself as a boat floating on very still water.

Shoulder stand

GOOD FOR:
mild upper-back/neck tension; depression

AVOID IF
you suffer from: severe upper-back/ neck tension; anxiety; very high blood pressure. Not suitable during menstruation.

SEE PP.94–5

Lie on your back with your head on the floor and a folded blanket under your shoulders. Draw your knees toward your chest. Place your hands flat on the floor by your sides and press down with your arms to lift your hips off the floor. Roll up high enough to tuck your hands into your low back and slide them down a little further – to the ribcage, if possible. Keep your elbows drawn tightly together and let your chest come toward your chin as you lift your body higher. Hold this pose for 4 to 12 breaths. Gently roll back down and lie flat for a few moments.

NOTES

Shoulder stand is an inverted pose that brings all kinds of positive tonic effects to the body. It is said to help stimulate the immune system and relieve bloating, feelings of sluggishness and depression. It is, however, a strong pose and must be treated with due respect. Don't do it if your neck or shoulders feel very tense – it may make them feel worse or even cause damage. On the other hand, if the tension is mild, shoulder stand may well relieve it. You will have to experiment a little to know what is right for you. Focus on the strong lifting in the back surface of the body and the overall sense of rising. The pose is a tonic for the mind as well as the body. It stimulates and calms in equal measure. You should feel alert but at peace after practising it.

Head to knee

GOOD FOR: hamstrings and low back; hip flexibility; breath awareness

TAKE CARE IF you suffer from: acute low-back pain

SEE P.93

Sit on the floor with your left leg outstretched and your right foot against your left thigh. Lengthen your left leg and draw your toes up toward you, so the leg feels energetic and strong. As you inhale, raise your arms overhead, lengthening your whole body. As you exhale, fold yourself forward over your leg, placing your hands on the floor on either side of your leg. Stay for 3 to 6 breaths. On each inhalation you make, slightly lengthen your body, and on each exhalation, gently relax forward a little more. Repeat on the other side.

NOTES

This pose is great for stretching the whole of the back surface of the body and gently massaging the internal organs. It also promotes hip flexibility and makes one very conscious of the effect of the breath as movement in the spine and torso as a whole. Don't try to get your head toward your knee at all costs – despite the name of the pose, this is not the aim! Encourage yourself to lengthen your body as much as you can and, above all, keep the pose gentle and relaxed. Much of the stiffness you will feel in this pose is owing to tension in muscles that need to be relaxed rather than pushed hard. Seated forward bends are introspective poses, making them particularly difficult to perform when we do not wish to see ourselves as we really are.

Tailor

GOOD FOR:
period pain; cystitis;
constipation

TAKE CARE IF
you have a groin strain
or a sprained ankle

SEE PP.96–7

Sit with the soles of your feet together and knees out to the sides. Place your hands on your feet with the thumbs pressed gently into the insides of the balls of your feet. Inhale fully and lengthen your spine, supporting it well with your belly muscles. As you exhale, gently fold your body forward. Rest your elbows on your calves or thighs, if they reach easily, and press them softly into your legs. Keep your shoulders soft and broad – don't be tempted to hunch them. Breathe steadily and evenly throughout. Try to hold the pose for 6 to 10 breaths.

NOTES

The deep opening in the hip sockets that this pose provides is invaluable. Tailor pose also stimulates the lower-abdominal organs and the nerves around the sacral area of the spine. It is a versatile posture and can be practised either in a strong way or in a very passive form (see p.97). Before you attempt the pose, experiment with the distance your feet are from your body. Try to find a point that is comfortable to begin working from. If your feet are very tucked in, you may find that your back rounds to compensate. You should avoid this, because it is important that you are able to sit up straight in the pose with ease.

Lying twist

GOOD FOR:
mild low-back pain; fatigue; tension and stress

SEE P.98

Lie on your back and tuck your knees very gently toward your chest. Then on an exhalation, drop both your knees over to your right side, allowing them to relax completely. Let your arms rest on the floor by your sides, palms up, and close your eyes. Allow all the muscles in your body to relax – including your tongue and your feet! Take 2 to 6 breaths in the pose and then inhale to lift your legs back to the centre and repeat on the other side. Repeat the whole exercise twice – or more if you have time.

NOTES

Twisting poses like this one are very beneficial for the spine. They also help to deepen your breathing and free pent-up tension in the body. All twists in yoga are reputed to release blockages and help us move on to new pastures. This is a great pose to practise if you feel yourself hanging on to something and unable to let go. Ensure that you really do relax while in the twist; it is easy for a little tension in your legs to persist if you are not vigilant.

Bridge

GOOD FOR:
neck and shoulder
tension; stress;
depression

TAKE CARE IF
you suffer from: very
weak knees or back;
extreme anxiety;
panic attacks

 SEE P.99

Lie on your back with knees bent and feet flat to the floor, parallel and hip-width apart. On an in-breath, lift your hips. Now clasp your hands behind you and push your knuckles toward your heels, lifting your hips a little higher. Draw your shoulder blades tightly under you and make your legs strong and steady. Stay for 2 to 6 breaths, then, on an out-breath, unclasp your hands, spread your arms and lower yourself to the floor. Try to lay each bone in your spine down one at a time, touching your waist down before your buttocks. Repeat 2 to 4 times.

NOTES

Bridge pose is a gentle but effective back-bending posture that really helps to alleviate tension in the shoulders, neck and upper back. Done with care and attention to the breath, it can correct poor posture habits very quickly. Try to keep both your feet well grounded throughout – especially your big toes, which tend to want to lift from the floor. To tuck your shoulder blades underneath you, you may need to rock from side to side. Explore the possible movements of the breath, allowing it to seep into your chest area to help to open it out. Keep your tailbone moving upward all the time to make your low back long and strong. Bridge, like most back bends, helps us to be open to the world around us and to get things into perspective when we can't see the wood for the trees.

CHAPTER 3:
Easy Solutions

No two people are the same. Different people will find a yoga pose easy, challenging or impossible depending on their unique body shape and condition. If you are finding any of the postures in Chapter 2 hard work, have a look at the following pages for a modification or variation to suit you. Understanding why you find a pose difficult can help you reach a solution. So, at the end of the chapter there is some basic anatomical information – to show how poor postural habits contribute to problems like back pain, and how yoga can help.

Correctly performed, a yoga pose should have an equal balance of grace and strength, stillness and energy, ease and security. If you have to strain to get into a pose, it has lost its integrity and you need to modify it to suit your body. Treat this chapter as a troubleshooting complement to Chapter 2 – come back to it over and over again as you and your yoga practice evolve.

How to modify a posture

Every yoga pose has various modifications that help make it easier to do or more beneficial. On the following pages I suggest a range of options that you might like to try. In each case the modifications are arrived at by identifying the "essence" of the posture. Start with the variations I have suggested and when you feel confident, explore your own.

Approach every posture with an inquiring mind and good observational attention and you will be able to personalize your practice very effectively. Don't be afraid to experiment, you won't do yourself any harm if you are careful.

Every pose should present a little bit of a challenge but this should be well within your control. You should not need to hold your breath and grit your teeth in order to stay in the posture. For example, suppose you are in Bridge pose, your legs feel wobbly and your low back aches when you try to hold the pose too long. You also notice that your breathing is very shallow and your chest feels compressed. In this case modify the amount of time you spend in the pose, inhaling to lift the hips up and exhaling to relax them back down onto the floor, repeating several times. This is easier than holding the hips up for, say, 6 consecutive breaths. Pay particular attention to the way the spine leaves and re-contacts the floor. You don't need to go very high, a gentle lift will do.

Now add a gentle arm movement to loosen your chest. Bring the arms overhead or to your sides at shoulder level as you inhale and bring them down as you exhale. Try out different variations until you you find one that is a bit of a challenge but does not cause a strain. If the extra arm movements make it too hard for you, just keep the arms by your sides.

STILLNESS OR MOVEMENT: Two simple ways to modify a pose are to practise it statically, staying in the pose for several breaths, or dynamically, going in to and out of the pose several times. The two different approaches yield different results. On the whole, the dynamic method is a little easier if you feel stiff or find the pose difficult. Once you feel confident try holding the pose for a long time.

PRIORITIZE THE SPINE: In almost every pose, the action of the spine is the main point of focus. If you need to change the arm or leg position so that it is easier to get the spine to bend or twist or become straight, then do.

SAFETY POINTS: Before you start, bear in mind the following considerations. Never use a block or cushion under your head in Shoulder stand or Bridge pose (under your shoulders is fine) as this puts additional pressure on your neck.

In standing poses, make sure your knees are tracking straight over the toes and not flopping to the side. And never jump, throw or bounce yourself into any pose. Everything should be done slowly and under control.

Forward bend
SOLUTIONS

Forward bends are often difficult at first because many of us suffer from stiffness in the low back and backs of the legs. No forward bend should be painful in your low back: a deep stretch in the backs of the legs is OK, but pain in the back is not. Go gently and slowly.

target position

SEE PP.30–31

❌ PROBLEM: **It's not too bad, but I can't keep my legs straight or my torso relaxed, and I can't touch the floor.**

✔ SOLUTION: **Bend your knees as much as you need to make your chest soft and relaxed. Bring your hands to your shins if they don't touch the floor.**

✗ PROBLEM: It feels impossible to relax or bend forward lower than to touch my knees.

✓ SOLUTION: Use a wall to help you. Press your hands into the wall about shoulder-width apart and straighten your legs, taking your feet a few inches apart. Try to lengthen your back from tailbone to head; don't let your head sag between your arms. Hold for 3 to 8 breaths.

✗ PROBLEM: My body will get into the forward bend, but I just can't relax!

✓ SOLUTION: Here is a lovely way to practise a forward bend with support. Sit on the edge of a chair and relax forward over a bolster or big cushion. Easy!

Warrior

SOLUTIONS

Problems with this pose can be caused by weakness or stiffness or both. Practice will pay off. Look out for the positioning of your feet. Your front foot must be strong and stable. The instep of your back foot must lift – pushing the outer edge of your heel down and keeping your leg really straight will help.

target position

SEE PP.32–3

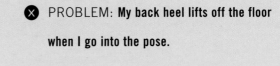

✕ PROBLEM: **My back heel lifts off the floor when I go into the pose.**

✓ SOLUTION: **Place a block under your heel, and press your heel firmly into the block.**

① ②

✕ PROBLEM: My neck, throat and chest feel very tense and I can't breathe easily/It's just too difficult!

✔ SOLUTION (STEP 1): Assume the starting foot and leg position described for warrior pose (the knee bend could be a little shallower). Inhale, lifting your arms to the position shown, keeping your chest wide and your shoulders soft.

✔ SOLUTION (STEP 2): As you exhale, bend forward, bringing your hands to the floor either side of your foot and relaxing your head and neck completely. Inhale to come up again. Repeat 2 to 4 times on each side.

Side lunge

SOLUTION

This pose is fairly taxing in many ways. Despite this it should not become rigid and tense. Instead, opt for a slightly easier approach and stay in the pose for a few more breaths until you have the strength to try the whole thing in full.

target position

SEE PP.34–5

✗ PROBLEM: **The pose is too strenuous to hold for long, or even to get into with ease.**

✓ SOLUTION: **Keep your knee bent as much as you can. Place your hand, rather than your forearm, on your thigh, and your other hand on your hip. Concentrate on the strength of your legs and the uplift in your low belly, opening your chest out as much as you can.**

Triangle

SOLUTION

A common mistake with this pose is to reach too far
down your leg, thus causing the chest to roll forward
and the hips to push backward. Try to make your
torso absolutely upright before you stretch across,
so you are bending strictly sideways only. Look
forward if looking up makes your neck ache.

**target
position**

SEE PP.36–7

⊗ PROBLEM: I can't reach down as far as
my shin.

⊘ SOLUTION: Bring your hand onto your thigh
just above your knee (not on it). Place your
other hand on your hip and concentrate on
keeping the rolling of your chest open and
your legs strong and firm.

Standing twist
SOLUTIONS

If you notice that you are holding your breath as you do the twist, try to stay in the pose for a couple of breaths, keeping your breathing very steady and relaxed. This will help you to improve flexibility in your chest and to increase your stamina. As always, try to go with the breath – not fight it.

target position

SEE PP.38–9

❌ PROBLEM: I can't get my hand down toward my ankle *and* twist *and* keep my legs straight.

✔ SOLUTION: Bend the knee toward which you are twisting. Place your hand on your hip rather than taking it right up overhead and focus on the twisting action in your torso.

✕ PROBLEM: **I'm finding it impossible to keep my spine extended in the twist/My back's rounding a lot, chin coming down to chest.**

✓ SOLUTION: **Place your hand on a chair. The additional support will help to make it possible to lengthen your spine, giving a better rotation, and you can still work your legs fully.**

✕ PROBLEM: **My legs feel too tight and/or weak to do the twist for more than a few seconds.**

✓ SOLUTION: **Try doing the twist on a chair. Sit sideways on the chair and, on an out-breath, turn your torso, holding the back of the chair with both hands. Stay for 3 to 6 breaths and then repeat on the other side.**

Mighty pose
SOLUTION

The backs of the legs can feel very tight in this pose, which is why you may be able to bend your knees only a little way before your heels lift off the floor. Also, if your knees tend to knock together or bow outward, you could try holding a block between them to keep them properly aligned.

target position

SEE PP.40–41

❌ PROBLEM: **My heels leave the floor as I go into the pose and it feels very wobbly!**

✅ SOLUTION: **Place a block under your heels, and come down into the squatting position as far as you can while keeping your heels down. For additional ease, place your elbows inside your knees and keep the palms of your hands together. Try to stay for a few breaths.**

Dancer

SOLUTION

Your balance can be affected by a number of things – for example, inner ear problems, a head cold, bunions or painful feet. Balancing skill generally deteriorates as we age and also during pregnancy. If you find it hard to balance, practise facing a wall for extra security, then it is there if you need it.

target position

SEE PP.42–3

❌ PROBLEM: **I can't catch hold of my foot behind me.**

✔️ SOLUTION: **Holding a belt in one hand, face a wall and put your other hand on it to help you to balance. Now use the belt to catch your foot. Shorten the belt to the minimum length required to enable you to do the pose. See if you can take your hand away from the wall and balance free.**

Cat

SOLUTION

Cat pose is quite accessible to most people, so what I have offered here is more of a variation than a solution. If Cat pose hurts your knees, kneel on a folded blanket to pad them a little. Other than that, most difficulties with the pose will be resolved by careful, regular practise.

original position

SEE PP.44–5

✕ PROBLEM: **I can do Cat pose – now I want something similar to vary my yoga practice.**

✓ SOLUTION: **This balancing variation of Cat pose develops core strength and stability. From an all-fours position, stretch out your left leg and then your right arm to make a strong diagonal line. Use your abdominal strength to hold the balance.**

Child
SOLUTION

Using props can really help you get into this pose if you are struggling with it. However, if despite all the props you still find it uncomfortable you could practise instead Knees to chest pose (see pp.54–5), which provides many of the same benefits while putting a little less strain on the hips.

target position

SEE PP.48–9

✕ PROBLEM: My head doesn't touch the floor/My legs are uncomfortable/The tops of my feet hurt.

✓ SOLUTION: Place a block or two underneath your head and a rolled-up mat or blanket under your ankles. You may also need an additional block or cushion between your hips and your heels.

Dog
SOLUTIONS

Like the Forward bends, Dog pose can be hard if your low back and hamstrings are stiff. It can also be a challenge if your shoulders are stiff, either through underuse and tension or because the muscles have become strong and bulky. Try these variations if you are finding the pose hard work.

target position

SEE PP.46–7

❌ PROBLEM: **My back is rounding and my legs are killing me!**

✓ SOLUTION: **Bend your knees. Let your heels come off the floor and concentrate on lifting your hips upward and drawing your chest toward your shins to stretch your spine.**

PROBLEM: My neck feels tense and my shoulders are hunched up, but I can straighten my spine OK.

SOLUTION: Try placing a large, firm cushion, a bolster or blocks under your head and relax your face, shoulders and neck as much as possible in the pose.

PROBLEM: I can't put that much weight on my wrists without them hurting/I don't like being upside down.

SOLUTION: This variation opens the shoulders and chest without inverting the body. Kneel close to a wall with your knees spread. Place your hands a little more than shoulder-width apart on the wall and rest your forehead on the wall. Breathe deeply for 4 to 8 breaths.

Shoulder stretch

SOLUTION

This pose needs a nice stable base, which would ideally be a kneeling position. But if this is uncomfortable, then try kneeling using a block (or a big book) to sit on, or, if your knees hurt when you kneel, you can always do this pose standing, or sitting on the edge of a kitchen-type chair.

target
position

SEE PP.50–51

ⓧ PROBLEM: **I can't get my hands to touch behind my back.**

✓ SOLUTION: **Use a belt to help you. Hold it in your top hand and let it hang down your back. Grasp the belt with your lower hand.**

Cobra

SOLUTION

As Cobra is unlikely to present any problems, I suggest here a similar pose, which would be a nice variation or addition to your sequence. It creates a diagonal stretch across the body, which is good for maintaining strength along the full length of the spine and for toning the abdominal organs.

original position

SEE PP.52–3

⊗ PROBLEM: I'm looking for a pose similar to Cobra, but that develops my low back.

✓ SOLUTION: Try Half-locust pose, which gives an asymmetrical upper-back movement. Lie on your front with your arms stretched out in front of you. Inhale and lift your head, chest, left arm and right leg a couple of inches off the floor. While exhaling, bring them gently back down. Repeat both sides 3 to 4 times.

Knees to chest

SOLUTION

If you are really struggling with this pose, practise a simple lying position first for a few days (see pp.110–11). Otherwise, try the instructions below. Remember that paying attention to your breathing is more important than being able to move your knees a long way toward your chest (see notes, p.54).

target position

SEE PP.54–5

⊗ PROBLEM: **It's really hard to catch hold of my knees at all and my chin is lifting up, making my neck arch.**

✓ SOLUTION: **Place a block underneath your head to help to lengthen your neck.**

Leg lifts

SOLUTION

Leg lifts look deceptively easy, but people with stiffness in their low back, hips and/or legs or weak abdominal muscles may find them difficult. This modification is a great way to ease tension in preparation for the full pose and it is also a really nice exercise in its own right.

target position

SEE PP.56–7

✕ PROBLEM: I can't lift my legs as high as I'm supposed to and still breath smoothly.

✓ SOLUTION: Do one leg at a time. Leave one foot on the floor with the knee bent and lift your other leg up, while stretching your arms out over your head and breathing in. On your out-breath, bring your leg back down and your arms to your sides. Repeat with your other leg.

Boat
SOLUTION

Boat pose requires quite a bit of strength. If it feels impossible at first, don't give up. Try to hold the pose for just a few breaths, then have a little rest and try again. You will quickly build up your stamina with these short repetitions. To help you balance, you could also try focusing your gaze on a fixed point across the room.

target position

SEE PP.58–9

❌ PROBLEM: **I'm not strong enough to hold the pose for longer than a few seconds.**

✔ SOLUTION: **Use your arms to help you initially – just focus on lifting your chest, staying high up on your sitting bones and not letting your back curve.**

Head to knee

SOLUTION

Tightness in the low back and legs can make this pose feel like very hard work indeed: it is made significantly easier by using a block under your hips. You could also lay a bolster across your thigh and rest your head on it as you bend forward, which feels nice if you suffer from tension in your upper back and neck.

target position

SEE PP.62–3

❌ PROBLEM: **It's very hard to sit up straight in this position, let alone bend forward.**

✅ SOLUTION: **Use a block to lift your hips a little. Just practise sitting up straight to begin with, then add the forward bend when you are ready. Hooking a strap around your foot can help when you come to bend forward.**

Shoulder stand
SOLUTIONS

This pose must be handled carefully, because it is demanding and has strong effects. If you are unsure about your technique or have relevant health problems, consult a qualified teacher before trying the full pose. Meanwhile, these variations may offer good alternatives or just a softer style of practice.

target position

SEE PP.60–61

X PROBLEM: Although I can get into the posture reasonably easily, my neck/head/chest feels under too much pressure.

✓ SOLUTION: Add more padding under your shoulders and elbows by using a couple of folded blankets or a platform made out of four foam blocks. Don't use cushions, as they are too squashy. Support your body with your hands and let your legs come forward a little.

❌ PROBLEM: **I just can't get into the pose!/ It really hurts my neck.**

✔ SOLUTION: **Place a bolster (not pictured) against a wall. Initially, rest your legs up the wall and your hips on the bolster. Then walk your feet up the wall far enough to get your hands tucked under your hips. Stay in this pose for a few breaths and then come down gently.**

❌ PROBLEM: **I don't want to go upside down at all (variation to use for extreme stress or anxiety and during menstruation).**

✔ SOLUTION: **Just lie with your legs stretched up a wall for a few minutes. This is a great pose to do when you need to change gear, say from work mode to family mode – it is really refreshing and relaxing.**

Tailor
SOLUTIONS

Here are a variety of ways to practise Tailor pose in order to increase hip flexibility. The first (this page) is a modification of the pose given in Chapter 2. The other two versions (opposite) give you ways of doing the pose entirely passively, which will enable you to relax and open the hip sockets.

target position

SEE PP.64–5

⊗ PROBLEM: **When I try to sit up straight, my back rounds.**

___

✓ SOLUTION: **Use a block or firm cushion under your hips to help straighten your spine.**

①   ②

❌ PROBLEM: **My back and legs feel very stiff in the sitting position (1).**

✔ SOLUTION: **Try a reclining version of the pose. Place a block under your head and a large cushion under each of your knees. A long belt looped under your low back and feet helps to support the pose. Close your eyes and stay in the pose for 3 to 8 minutes.**

❌ PROBLEM: **My low back and legs feel very stiff in the sitting position (2).**

✔ SOLUTION: **Again lying down, bring one foot onto the opposite thigh, letting the knee turn outward (prop it up with a cushion if necessary). Stay for a minute or so on each side and then try the first reclining solution (left).**

Lying twist
SOLUTION

One of the simplest ways to vary a twisting pose is
to reposition your legs. If you find the twist hard, try
starting with your feet flat on the floor, and your
knees bent instead of tucked in toward your chest.
Let your knees drop to the floor from this position.
The twist will be less strong and lower in your back.

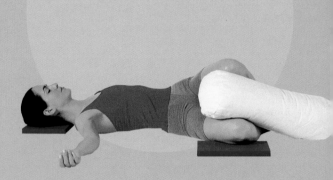

target position

SEE PP.66–7

❌ PROBLEM: **It hurts my back/I can't get my
legs to relax to the floor.**

✔ SOLUTION: **Make it easier by placing a thick
cushion or bolster between your knees and a
small block under your head. You may want an
additional cushion or block under your lower
knee as well.**

Bridge
SOLUTION

Bridge can feel like a strain in your low back if you are not engaging the muscles in your low abdomen properly. Tilting your tailbone upward should correct this problem. You may need to squeeze your buttocks together quite hard to feel this tilt at first. The pose should feel easy and soft overall and not a strain.

**target
position**

SEE PP.68–9

❌ PROBLEM: **It hurts my low back/It feels unstable.**

✓ SOLUTION: **Practise dynamically. Clasp your hands behind your back. Inhale and, firmly tilting your tailbone upward, lift your hips as far as you can without discomfort. Roll straight back down on your out-breath, releasing your hands, and repeat 4 to 6 times.**

Anatomy of the spine

It is important to remember that the skeleton, especially the spine, is a living mechanism. It is not a dry, brittle object but a dynamic structure full of blood vessels and fluids, constantly repairing and regenerating itself.

The spine is made up of 7 cervical (neck) vertebrae, 12 thoracic (chest) vertebrae, 5 lumbar (low back) vertebrae, the sacrum and the coccyx (vestigial tail, referred to in this book as the "tailbone").

Each bony vertebra is separated from its neighbour by a disc, a pad of tough gelatinous tissue that ensures smooth movement between adjacent vertebra and acts as a cushion against jarring movements. The spinal cord runs down a central channel for the entire length of the spine and is protected from injury by the bones. The nerves that control the body radiate out from the spinal cord. The large nerves that branch down from the sacral area into the legs are known as the sciatic nerves. Many people suffer from the severe pain caused when one of these nerves is pressurized by the surrounding tissues.

The spine has a series of natural curves. These are necessary to help the spine to absorb the shock caused by movements such as walking, running and jumping. The curves also make it possible to balance the considerable weight of the head on top of the spine with minimum muscular effort. It is quite common to find that, through poor posture or lack of muscular strength, the spinal curves are either exaggerated or almost lost. In either case the result can be painful and/or create a lack of mobility. Every person's spine is unique and the exact degree of healthy curvature will vary considerably from person to person.

Yoga postures require the spine to perform a huge variety of movements, bending and twisting in all directions. These movements keep the spine strong and well nourished.

The different shapes and sizes of the vertebrae give the spine good backward flexibility at the low back, more rotational capacity in the chest region and a wide range of motion in the neck. Regular yoga helps to enhance spinal mobility.

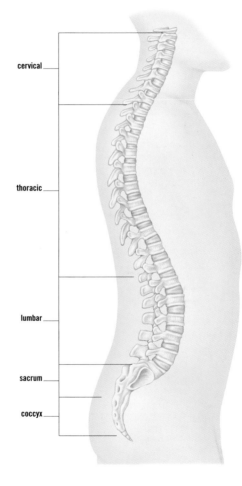

cervical

thoracic

lumbar

sacrum

coccyx

Anatomy of the hamstrings and low back

The pictures on the opposite page show the arrangement of the hamstrings, the muscles in the backs of the legs, and their effect on posture involving the pelvis and low back. The great majority of beginners find that this area is stiff when they first start yoga. It is quite normal (though lamentable) for an adult beginner to find it impossible to sit on a floor with legs outstretched and spine upright.

There are some factors in the arrangement of these muscles that make them liable to stiffen up in the first place and then to stay that way if you don't do anything about it. The hamstring muscles extend over two joints – the hip joint and the knee. This is why in situations where you are stretching your hamstrings you will find bending your knees a little relieves the stretch. It is also why you'll find that if you straighten your legs completely, for example, when sitting on the floor with legs outstretched in front of you, your back will have to round if the muscles are tight.

Once you understand such connections it is easy to see why regularly stretching and lengthening these muscles is important. In the long run, the increased flexibility you gain will make a whole range of movements much easier and more comfortable to perform.

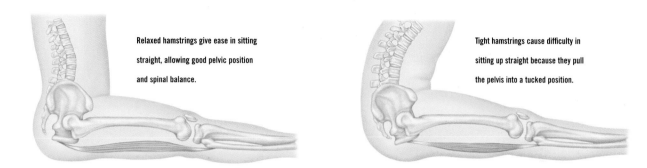

Relaxed hamstrings give ease in sitting straight, allowing good pelvic position and spinal balance.

Tight hamstrings cause difficulty in sitting up straight because they pull the pelvis into a tucked position.

This picture shows the group of thigh muscles known collectively as the hamstrings (back view). By carrying out regular leg stretching exercises you can help keep the hamstrings relaxed and so aid suppleness and mobility.

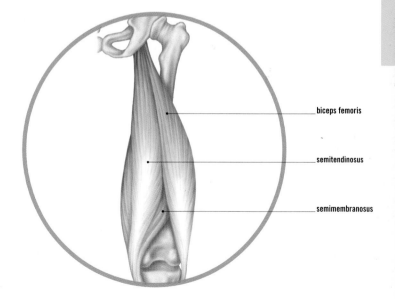

biceps femoris

semitendinosus

semimembranosus

Anatomy of the skeletal muscles

Here is an atlas of the body showing the main skeletal muscles. You do not need to know the names of the muscles you are using in order to feel them working. But for many students of yoga, a visual representation of the muscles and their location helps them to conceptualize what is happening internally when they move and stretch in a posture.

Twisting and forward bending poses compress and then release the internal organs, flooding them with fresh blood and nutrients. Back bending and side bending poses extend and then release them. The connective tissue that holds all the organs in place needs to be kept healthy and strong too, and yoga helps to do that. In yoga, the effect of a posture on the internal organs is all-important. For example, postures performed lying on your front, such as Cobra pose, produce quite a bit of pressure on the internal organs. These postures provide a positive way of massaging the organs to increase blood and fluid supply to them, and help them to expel waste materials and so ensure their continued healthy functioning.

Training regimes that focus on working one muscle or muscle group more than others tend to cause imbalance. The whole body should be worked evenly for optimum health.

FRONT

BACK

trapezius

deltoid

pectoralis major

latissimus dorsi

biceps brachii

serratus anterior

triceps brachii

internal intercostal

external abdominal oblique

internal abdominal oblique

transversus abdominis

gluteus medius

rectus abdominis

iliopsoas

sartorius

quadriceps femoris

gastrocnemius

soleus

trapezius

levator scapulae

deltoid

rhomboideus major

teres minor

teres major

triceps brachii

erector spinae

serratus posterior

latissimus dorsi

external abdominal oblique

gluteus medius

gluteus maximus

semitendinosus

biceps femoris

semimembranosus

} hamstrings

sartorius

gastrocnemius

soleus

CHAPTER 4:
Easy Relaxation

Yoga is famous for its stress-relieving properties. In this chapter we look at three aspects of yoga that are especially important for bringing the body and mind into a state of calm – relaxation, breathing and meditation. All of the exercises in this chapter work best if they are preceded by a series of gentle yoga poses to help to bring the physical body into a calm/alert state. However, if time is short you will find exercises in this chapter that will help to promote a sense of peaceful ease in just a few minutes – a kind of first aid for stress!

Relaxation is something we can train ourselves to do at will and the breathing techniques of yoga allow us to first observe and then control our emotional states to great effect. Meditation and concentration offer an extraordinary tool for changing our lives in a positive way. What's more, it is so easy to start. You don't need any special circumstances or equipment to learn to calm mind and body – simply the will to do it!

What happens when you relax

GOOD FOR:
everybody

TAKE CARE IF
you are depressed

Relaxation is vital to our health and well-being. Although we all need a little "stress" to get going, most of us now feel we are under too much pressure, at least some of the time. Relaxation is a "natural" state, but it is something we have to re-learn if we have got used to constant tension. To function to their maximum potential, both the mind and body need to be fully relaxed from time to time.

Various physical changes occur in the body during deep relaxation. Muscles relax, the digestive system and salivary glands work freely, and the heart rate and breathing slow. Also body temperature drops quite noticeably during relaxation, so you should practise in a warm room, or cover yourself with a blanket.

In a state of deep relaxation the mind is still, but fully conscious. Most beginners find that when they first try relaxation exercises either their mind is buzzing or they fall asleep! After a little practice one can move to a point of stillness between being fully alert and being sleepy, where you are neither daydreaming nor drifting into complex thought processes.

In order to reach this state of mental stillness, we need to give the mind something simple to focus on, like rhythmical breathing or counting. Music, which can be relaxing at first, is a source of stimulation. Eventually, these exercises should be done in silence.

If possible, practise postures first, followed by breathing exercises and then relaxation and/or meditation. This order offers the best results because each step prepares you for the next. The breath becomes slower and more even after practising postures, and mental focus is improved by breathing practices.

By using physical poses that divert your attention away from the world around you and make you fully conscious of your body and the voluntary control of muscle you start a steady process of increasing interiorization. Then you deepen your attention to your breathing where, as you work through the exercises, you grow aware of minute changes at a physiological and emotional level. Finally, relaxation and meditation allow you to complete the process and become physically and mentally still.

Relaxation, meditation and breathing exercises require no physical exertion so they are ideal for anyone who is injured, unwell or who lacks the time or energy to do postures. Anyone can benefit from these practices and, although they take some time to perfect, the principles on which they are based and the techniques they employ are easy to follow.

Rarely, people report that when they try relaxation, breathing or meditation they feel anxious or panic. If this happens to you then stop at once and just practise postures for a few weeks before trying again. Sometimes one needs to develop a better foundation in the stability and clarity that postures give before moving to the more interior-focused exercises.

Rest and quiet contemplation

Deep, conscious relaxation is called *yoga nidra* (yogic sleep), a state in which the nervous system can repair and collect itself. The technique is simple. Find a quiet, warm, well ventilated room. Cover yourself in a blanket (your temperature drops in deep relaxation). Lie on the floor (not the bed, where you may fall asleep!) and close your eyes. If your chin sticks up put a small cushion or book under your head so that your face is level. Place your feet a little apart so the thighs aren't touching. If your back is uncomfortable, bend the knees and put a rolled blanket under them, or put your feet flat on the floor. Place your hands 30cm (12in) from your sides, so the upper arm doesn't touch your sides, with palms upward.

TENSE AND RELEASE

Lift your right leg off the floor a little, tensing the muscles, then let it relax as you breathe out. Do the same with the left leg. Now repeat, tensing and releasing buttock muscles, abdominal muscles, chest, shoulders, arms, neck, face and scalp. Each time, tense the muscles for a few seconds and then release completely. Over the next few minutes it is important that you don't move at all, so get as comfortable as you can. Let your body rest.

Notice how you feel. Don't "try" to relax. Let your mind settle down and then start to rotate your awareness around your body. Become aware of your left foot, ankle, shin, knee, thigh, hip and the left side of your waist,

yoga nidra posture

chest, shoulder, upper arm, elbow, lower arm, wrist and hand. Repeat on the right.

Feel the back surface of your body on the floor, spreading out, heavy, warm. Feel the front surface of the body open out, heavy, warm. Take your awareness to the back of your neck and head, your forehead, eyelids, nose, mouth, cheeks, jaw, tongue, ears, throat, heart. Let your brain rest inside your skull, floating. Let the spine ripple along the floor, floating. Feel the breath moving in and out of the body, effortlessly. Even, steady breathing. Let the in-breath brush down your body from head to toe, let your out-breath brush back up from toes to head. Each breath is effortless, even and easy. Let yourself be here for a little while, effortlessly, quiet and peaceful. Slowly draw your awareness toward your surroundings. Listen to the sounds of the room and beyond. Become aware of the light level behind your eyelids, the sensation of the body resting on the floor, the air temperature against your skin. Then let yourself stretch, yawn and roll over onto your side for a few moments. Collect your thoughts. Sit up slowly. Sit quietly for a few moments, observe how you feel. Take this inner stability with you into your daily life.

Mind and breath connection

Our mental and emotional states are reflected in the way we breathe. Fear, excitement, anger and stress all affect the normal pattern of relaxed breathing. However, through the use of yoga breathing exercises we can change the way we feel mentally and emotionally. These changes can happen over the short term (calming you in a crisis) and over the long term on a subtle level (improving your general state of mind and emotional equilibrium).

The respiratory system is unusual among body systems as it is both involuntary (we continue to breathe without having to think about it consciously and carry on breathing while asleep, in a faint, or sedated) and voluntary (we can hold our breath, speed it up, slow it down and vary it in other different ways). This kind of control is not possible with, for example, the digestive or endocrine system. A side effect of being able to control the respiratory system is that we also lower the heart rate and blood pressure. The practice of relaxation and breathing go hand in hand.

If you want to calm your mind and your emotions quickly and efficiently then you need to be able to control your breathing. But this is not so easy because if your mind is telling your body that there is a panic situation, your breathing will leap into panic mode — shallow fast and chesty. A vicious circle then develops in which you feel unable to calm down or control your breathing.

Yoga breathing techniques make it possible to learn and practise breath control in order to master the mind and emotions so that they don't gallop off like a pack of wild horses leaving you floundering in their tracks!

The Sanskrit name for breathing exercises is *pranayama*. This is made up of two parts: *prana*, the "life-force" or energy that is moved by the breath, and *ayama*, which literally means to stretch or to control.

The basic techniques of *pranayama* allow us to regulate the four parts of a breathing cycle: inhalation, retention of the inhale, exhalation, and retention of the exhale. The overall aim is to deepen the breath, making it fuller, longer and finer or more subtle.

Devoting just a few minutes a day to yoga breathing can give amazing results. Indeed, even if you are enthusiastic about practising *pranayama* you should limit it to just one or two 3 to 10 minute practices a day. More could be a strain. It is of vital importance to maintain ease of breath at all costs. If you strain in a *pranayama* exercise then you risk stressing the emotions and your mental balance.

On the following pages you will find a few simple exercises. Even a very advanced yoga practitioner uses these simple exercises regularly to maintain their breath control. Practice for a few minutes daily if you can, preferably after practising some postures, which will help to prepare the body and mind.

Easy breathing exercises

These simple breathing exercises are best practised lying down. To start, put yourself in a comfortable position. If you feel that your chin is tilting upward you could place a small cushion or block beneath your head. Now bend your knees, placing your feet flat on the floor hip-width apart, and then let your knees rest against one another.

BREATH AWARENESS

In the following exercises, breathe through your nose throughout. Place your hands on your abdominal area and rest for a while as you feel the natural movement of the breath, the rise and fall of the body, and the slight natural pauses between exhale and inhale.

Without changing your normal breathing pattern deliberately, become aware of the duration of each breath, the depth of each breath and the quality of each breath. For example, is the breath rough or smooth, even or uneven, subtle or strong?

Notice the temperature of the air as it enters your nostrils and as it leaves. Stay with this for quite a long time, feel the sensation of letting yourself follow your breath mentally.

LENGTHEN THE BREATH

Now begin to let your breath lengthen. Count how long it takes you to breathe in and how long it takes you to breathe out. Begin to lengthen your exhalation steadily, adding a few more counts every four or five breaths until your exhale is 2–3 times as long as the inhale. (It might take you a while to work up to this.) At all times the breath should remain smooth and soft, never forced or strained. Continue for a few rounds, making your breath as long as you can without straining, and then gradually shorten it back down to your original count.

HUMMING-BEE BREATH

In this exercise you hum on your out-breath making a sound like a bee. It is so simple and yet so effective. The humming helps you to lengthen your out-breath and the vibration of the hum creates a wonderfully warming and soothing effect over the whole body. Try different pitches of humming to find one that feels really comfortable, and stay with it for a while. You can keep going for as long as you like, then end by making the hum quieter and quieter until you are silent and just feeling the afterglow of the vibration in the body.

easy breathing posture

More easy breathing exercises

Once you feel happy doing the breathing exercises lying down, try these simple seated exercises. Most people say that when they first begin to do yoga breathing sitting up they find their backs become tired or achy. This is one of the reasons why yoga places such an emphasis on postures to help to strengthen the spine enough to sit straight and breath deeply with ease for several minutes at a time.

If you can, sit cross-legged or in Adepts pose (shown below) with a small cushion or block underneath your hips. If you find that too uncomfortable, you could sit up straight on a chair with your hands resting on your thighs and feet firmly on the floor (see p.121).

adepts pose

THE VICTORIOUS BREATH: UJJAYI PRANAYAMA
Inhale and exhale through your nose, and softly close your throat a tiny amount so that you can regulate the pressure of the air passing through. It will make a gentle hissing sound as the breath passes. (You get a similar feeling

when you blow onto a mirror to steam it up, but in this case the breath comes through the nose and not the mouth.) The sound is very helpful, meditative and reassuring. It doesn't need to be loud, just consistent. (A bit like the sound of the "sea" that you hear when you put a shell to your ear.) You use slightly different muscles on the inhale and the exhale so they sound a bit different and you will feel the inhale a little higher in the throat than the exhale. Practise doing a few rounds of up to 8 breaths and then extend to 15 or 20 breaths at a time.

ANULOMA UJJAYI

In this technique you breathe in through both nostrils and out through alternate nostrils.

This has the effects of slowing your breathing down and calming the mind. It is an excellent remedy for times when you feel that everything is going too fast and you need to slow down! Use your right thumb to close your right nostril and exhale gently and slowly through the left nostril only. Now release your thumb and breathe in through both nostrils, using the *ujjayi* breath technique. Now close your left nostril using the ring and little fingers of your right hand and exhale through the right nostril only (no *ujjayi* technique on the exhalations). Release your fingers, inhale again, using *ujjayi* breathing through both nostrils. Repeat the whole exercise 6 to 8 times. Keep your breath gentle and soft throughout.

Easy meditation exercises

Meditation is the means through which a Yogi traditionally achieves a state of enlightenment or *samadhi*. Whether or not you hope to become enlightened, the practical benefits of a regular meditation practice can be huge. They include peace of mind, improved sleep, stress relief, better concentration and better health all round. Your success at meditation will be improved by the regular practice of postures, breathing techniques and relaxation exercises, which is why they're all steps on the yoga path.

The idea of meditating can seem a little daunting at first, especially as it can be hard to imagine or describe exactly what a state of meditation feels like. But don't let this put you off trying it out for yourself. Describing meditation, rather like describing sleep or love, is far more difficult than the practice itself. And also rather like sleep and love, meditation is an illusive state that is not brought about by willpower alone!

Solid, regular practice does help though. When people talk about doing regular meditation they understand that for a long time the practice will not be a "success". That is to say, this special state of mind is not achieved on every – or even most – occasions.

From time to time, a meditative state can be achieved accidentally in daily life, you just feel that you slip from concentration or contemplation into another realm altogether. This is not daydreaming or sleep, just a kind of stillness of mind, absolute absorption lasting from a few moments to a few minutes. The importance of regular practice of meditation is that you begin to be able to get into this state of mental clarity and stillness on demand.

This may take years to achieve, but the process of practising is beneficial in itself and the peace and stillness of the body and the willingness to try to quiet and open the mind eventually lead to the actuality. At this point it becomes a powerful tool, for a mind sharpened by meditation is capable of much more than one cluttered by the concerns of everyday life.

The good news is that all you need to meditate are a few minutes of spare time and the desire to have a go and see what happens!

PREPARING FOR MEDITATION

For the vast majority of Westeners, sitting crossed-legged on the floor is uncomfortable, at best. For many it is simply impossible. Do not despair – just because you can't sit on the floor doesn't mean you can't meditate!

The most important features of a seated position are that it should be still, and sustainable for at least 5 minutes without discomfort, the spine should be straight and well supported by the muscles of the torso, and the heavy weight of the head should be balanced on top of the spine so as to create the minimum strain on the skeletal muscles. Finally, the posture you choose must not be so comfortable that you fall asleep.

You can't successfully meditate lying down or slumped in a sofa. So the best solution for most of us is to use a chair. Choose one with a firm flat seat. Check that you can put your feet flat on the floor comfortably. Sit well forward on the seat with the spine long and free. Slightly draw the chin toward the throat to create a little extra length in the back of your neck. Let your hands rest on your lap.

Experiment to find the best position for your feet on the floor. The feet flat on the floor, about hip-width apart can feel nice and stable, but it also increases your awareness of the energy in the feet. Alternatively, try crossing your ankles. This may feel uncomfortable if your ankles are stiff (in which case revert back to the previous posture). Now let your hands rest on your thighs and relax all of the muscles in your face, neck and shoulders.

MIND AND BREATH MEDITATION

Take a few steady breaths, counting how long it takes you to breathe in and out. Keep counting and breathing until you feel quite still inside and then let go of the counting and try to stay mentally with the breath.

Each time you feel distracted, draw your attention back to the breath. Eventually, you may find yourself able to let go of the breath and allow the mind to be still. This takes time and don't be surprised if you find it impossible at first. It does come with practice.

seated posture
for meditation

SIMPLE MEDITATION

Here is another pre-meditation exercise based on a nursery rhyme that you may know mixed with the idea of "rotation of awareness of the body" (see Rest and quiet contemplation, pp.110–11). The principle is to attach the mind to something simple, in order to free it from the constant whirl it is usually performing. In the long run one can drop the "simple thing" you chose, in this case the nursery rhyme, and just let the mind "be". It is extraordinarily hard to imagine this state, let alone get to it! So let's start with the simple thing for now and see where that takes us.

Heads, shoulders, hips, knees, toes
Heads, shoulders, hips, knees, toes
Eyes, ears, mouth, throat
Eyes, ears, mouth, throat

Now sit quietly and go through the list in your head, naming each body part and letting each part relax as you go. There is nothing to do but go through the list quite slowly and steadily a few times. (Don't speed up!) If you start to feel very stable and centred just let the rhyme drop away and allow your mind to be still. That's it. Easy!

Using sound for relaxation

We live in a world full of sound: so full that we suffer from "noise pollution" and so polluted that we rarely experience quiet any more. The sounds made by traffic, aircraft and machines produce a background rumble that is overlaid by television, radio, music and voices. On a more subtle level, there is the constant hum of electrical appliances – such as the the computer, dishwasher and refrigerator.

Every sound is a pattern of vibration that can affect every particle of our bodies. Our bodies can even respond to vibrations that are too low- or high-pitched to be audible. Some vibrations can make us feel unwell, and others can make us feel better. According to Yogic tradition, the universe vibrates to a sound that is represented by the symbol ॐ. This symbol is usually transcribed as *om* or *aum* – the closest the human voice can get to the sound. It is said that a yogi who chants the sound of *om* eventually hears the sound of the universe vibrating within himself.

Sound has many roles to play in yoga. Chanting Sanskrit texts and reciting mantram is fundamental to traditional yoga instruction. These mantram, containing the essence of yoga teaching, are faithfully passed down from teacher to student. Great care is taken with pronunciation as each sound has its own unique vibration. Sanskrit itself is a "sacred" language in which every sound has special significance.

All societies use singing and chanting as a way of lifting the spirits, expressing deep emotion and marking special events. We chant in football stadiums and sing in pubs, and at birthday parties and so on. When you make rhythmical sounds the breath has to become rhythmical too. The combination of the control of the breath and the production of the vibration itself has a strongly uplifting effect on the whole system and is a powerful force for healing. If you feel gloomy, sing to yourself for five minutes and you may feel a lot better!

It really is impossible to learn the traditional Sanskrit chanting without the aid of an accomplished teacher but many of the same benefits of chanting can be gained through using simple sounds that have no meaning or significance in themselves. On the following pages I suggest ways to combine sounds such as humming with movements.

Before you start, turn off your phone and other electrical appliances – maybe even the refrigerator, just for 5 minutes – and enjoy the silence. Then make some real sound! Begin by sitting or lying down and try the Humming-bee breathing technique (see p.115).

Now add the following combined movement and sound exercises and see what works best for you. All of these exercises are effective when you are feeling tense or stressed. They release pent up energy and emotion and let the body find a comfortable level of vibration.

Simple sound

GOOD FOR:

stress and tension

This simple forward bend movement can be combined with a variety of sounds to help you become more aware of your breathing and eventually to have better control over it. The sounds themselves have a powerful effect, both energizing and relaxing at the same time.

You can experiment with the sounds suggested here as well as trying other sounds. The process of making sound and listening to it brings a basic form of concentration into your practice, which can then be followed through into meditation as and when you wish.

Experiment with sounds. Start with a hum and turn it into a vowal sound:

mmmm ... ah

mmmm ... oh

mmmm ... ee

mmmm ... oo

mmmm ... aye

Now reverse the pattern so that you start with the vowel sound and end with the humming sound:

ah ... mmmm

oh ... mmmm

ee ... mmmm

oo ... mmmm

aye ... mmmm

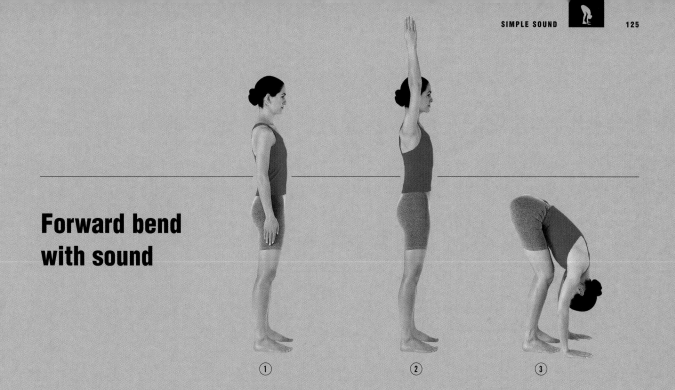

① ② ③

Forward bend with sound

Stand, feet a few inches apart and parallel. Allow your arms to hang by your sides and let the spine lengthen naturally (1). Inhale, lifting your arms overhead, keeping them shoulder-width apart (2). As you exhale, make a humming sound opening to an "ahh" as you come into a soft forward bend (to make it comfortable relax your knees as necessary; 3). Repeat 4 to 6 times, keeping the breath and the sound slow and steady. Experiment with other sounds until you find the best for you.

Bridge pose with sound

Here is another exercise in which you can experiment with sound and movement together. It is a variation of the Bridge pose described on p.68. However, in this case you should place most of the emphasis on the quality of the breath and sound and try not to think of it so much as a physical exercise. This is a deeply relaxing and refreshing practice that may possibly raise some deep-seated emotions to the surface. If this happens, just lie down quietly and let them pass before you come back up to a sitting position.

Lie on your back with knees bent and feet hip-width apart. Place your arms on the floor by your sides, palms facing down, and rest for a few breaths (1). Listen to your natural breathing rhythm. On an inhalation, lift your arms over your head until they relax onto the floor above you, bending your elbows enough to allow your whole arm to rest easily on the floor (2). As you exhale, make a "sooo" sound. Inhale again and lift your hips off the floor to make a gentle slope from knees to shoulders (3). As you exhale, lower the body to the floor, making the sound "maa" as you go. Inhale, and as you exhale bring the arms back down by your sides, making the sound "sooo". Repeat 4 to 6 times. Try switching the sounds – "maa", "sooo" then "maa". Rest for a few breaths, feeling the after-hum of the sound settle through your body.

CHAPTER 5:
Easy Yoga for Easy Sports

If you take part in sports or other physical leisure activity, which might be as varied as darts, tennis, football, bowling or dancing, then yoga can offer you a whole range of benefits to improve your performance and enhance your enjoyment. This is true for people competing at any level, from total beginner to professional athlete. Because yoga is concerned with the workings of the mind as well as the body it provides an ideal form of cross-training. You can deeply stretch and open areas that are tight; strengthen areas that are weak; and develop the positive mental attitude that will help you to succeed in your chosen activity. In this chapter we examine why yoga can help the sportsman and sportswoman mentally and physically and look at the kinds of yoga practice that would be most appropriate for a variety of pursuits, including tough contact sports, endurance activities such as running, and graceful racquet sports such as badminton.

Mind and movement

"Yoga citta vritti Nirodha"

—Yoga is the ability to focus the mind on a single point without distraction.

PATANJALI YOGA SUTRAS 1.2

The key difference between yoga and sports training is the quality of interior focus. In a sport you set yourself an external goal – 30 sit ups, running 100 metres, or whatever. In yoga the "goal" is complete and steady focus of the mind on the chosen point. During a yoga practice this point of focus is the awareness of the physical, emotional and mental response to postures. Carefully monitoring the processes attached to movement can help you to develop a highly refined practice on all levels.

Just thinking about a muscle movement or series of movements can have a positive effect on how you execute the movement in reality. Visualizations that encourage you to think of a muscle lengthening or opening or softening actually help the body to make that movement.

You can adapt the visualizations to suit your needs and practise them on their own or as part of a yoga session in order to improve the mind-body connection and gain real benefit. Athletes who visualize winning can win!

As an example, let's take a simple pose such as Cobra on p.52. Doing the posture mechanically will strengthen the muscles in the upper back. This is good, but we can do much better. As you begin, lying face down, feel the muscles in the body relax completely and listen to the steady rhythm of your breath. Keep your breathing steady as you move into the preparatory position. Notice the muscular changes in the body, notice any changes in the speed, depth or quality of your breathing.

As you inhale to lift the head and chest off the floor, feel the parts of the body that are supporting you in contact with the floor. Be aware of whether they are active (your leg muscles may have tensed to help you lift) or relaxed. Feel the palms of the hands spread open and in contact with the floor.

Now experience the opening action as the breath rises into the chest area. If you don't feel this, try imagining it first. This helps it to happen. (Lying on your front, the abdomen and diaphragm are restricted, so inhalation feels different from how it would on your back.)

As your exhalation begins, feel the process of softening the muscles as you bring the head and chest back to the floor. Be aware of which muscles move first, which are resisting the downward movement to slow it to the same pace as your breath. Feel the sensation of letting go completely when you reach the floor.

You will find that at first it is very difficult to maintain this acute level of awareness, particularly of the breath – as the mind is inclined to wander half way through. With a little practice you will be able to keep this level of work going throughout each exercise.

Yoga as cross-training

Yoga is an ideal tool for athletes and sports players of all standards to enhance their performance and deepen their understanding of their skills. Yoga improves concentration and develops the self-awareness and self-discipline needed to achieve in any sport. The postures can be arranged in countless ways for different effects. And as we have seen in previous chapters, yoga postures can be adapted to suit you individually. You can use yoga as cross-training in the following ways.

WARM-UP AND COOL-DOWN EXERCISES help to prepare the body gradually for further work. Yoga provides gentle preparation for further exercise. It works equally well after training or a sporting event by helping to restore the body to a natural state of equilibrium and assimilate the experience of training or competition. Yoga stretching as part of a cool-down routine can reduce post-exercise muscle soreness.

STIMULATING EXERCISES help to strengthen or prepare certain muscles groups. For example, yoga offers a safe and effective way to build up strength and flexibility in the ankles. Helpful poses are Balancing (see p.28), Dog (see p.46), Head to knee (see p.62) and Tailor (see p.64).

RELAXATION EXERCISES such as Tailor pose (see p.64), Shoulder stand variations (see p.94) and Deep relaxation (see p.110), help to relax certain muscles and body functions. The ability to relax a specific area, on demand, is vital for athletes. For example, the shoulders should swing freely when you run. You cannot run to your maximum potential if your shoulders are tense – you waste valuable energy and cause a mechanical and energetic blockage. Yoga helps you identify areas of tension and then release them.

CONCENTRATION EXERCISES develop the self-discipline and mental focus needed to succeed in sports. To be psychologically prepared for your game or event, practise self-study and acute self-observation through yoga. The introspective nature of yoga helps to build core mental strength that allows you to focus clearly even under pressure. This can be done using yoga postures, sound, breathing exercises, relaxation and meditation.

REGENERATION EXERCISES help speed recovery after injury or exertion. Yoga postures have a powerful restorative effect. If you are injured or have pushed your body to its limits, yoga poses can ease the body into movement again without strain and have the beneficial effect of conserving energy and restoring balance. Knees to chest (see p.54), Tailor (see p.64), Bridge (see p.68) and Shoulder stand variations (see p.94) may be especially helpful in bringing the body systems back into balance.

COMPENSATION EXERCISES make allowances for muscle imbalance caused by a particular sports technique. For sports such as golf, tennis, or baseball where there is a great deal of asymmetric movement, you will need to focus on yoga poses that work the body asymmetrically to help you to re-balance. These include Warrior (see p.32), Side lunge (see p.34), Triangle (see p.36), Standing twist (see p.38), Dancer (see p.42), and Head to knee (see p.62). If your sport is basically symmetrical, such as cycling, running or basketball, you could use any symmetrical poses that run counter to the poses you adopt in your normal training regime. So, if your sport involves a lot of forward bending movements (as rowing and cycling do) you could compensate by doing gentle yoga back bends, such as Dancer (see p.42), Cobra (see p.52) and Bridge (see p.68) poses.

SUPPLEMENTAL EXERCISES provide a good way to broaden the range and quality of movement offered in sports training. It can be very refreshing just to do something different. For example, after regular weight training or swimming, yoga lets you feel your body operate in a different way. You will notice that your body is very capable in some areas and feels really restricted in others. You will be able to assess the effects of your yoga practice on your normal training and performance.

Easy yoga for running/football

Running, and team sports that involve a lot of running, such as football, strengthen the legs, but work less effectively on the upper body. So yoga postures that stretch the legs and build complementary strength in the upper body and spine are of use in balancing out your training.

Dog pose (see p.46) is of particular importance as it does all three things! It actively stretches the hamstrings and calves. It strengthens the upper body, and both strengthens and stretches the spine.

Dancer pose (see p.42) opens out the thighs and causes a slight back-bending action which is of benefit. The Squatting pose (pictured right) encourages flexibility in the knees, hips and ankles – essential for maintaining the

shock-absorbing powers of the legs – as well as opening and lengthening the low back.

Warming up or cooling down routines could include these poses – held steadily for at least 3 to 4 breaths (and preferably a good deal longer) with several repetitions of each pose.

squatting pose

Easy yoga for racquet sports

All racquet sports are inherently one-sided. The racquet arm is worked much harder and in a way that is different from the other arm, leading to muscular imbalance. This is sometimes quite clearly visible where players develop one arm that is noticeably larger and stronger than the other. In addition, although the body repeatedly twists as it follows through after the active arm it will not twist in the other direction as regularly, as far, or with such force during a match. Therefore yoga poses that help players to compensate for the imbalance are important.

shoulder stretch, p.50

Also vital are poses that give strength and tone to the low back (which is the point of strain of the twisting action). Shoulder muscles tend to lose flexibility as they get stronger so postures that encourage shoulder flexibility should be incorporated into your practice on a regular basis. The ankles and knees need to be kept flexible and strong as well, so poses that work on these areas are also necessary. It

dog pose, p.46

would be beneficial to follow a training session with a series of poses that include Cat (see p.44), Dog (see p.46), Shoulder stretch (see p.50) and Bridge (see p.68) poses. A longer routine could include Warrior (see p.32) and Triangle (see p.36) poses and Standing twist (see p.38). Overall, a yoga session can provide complementary training to help to create equilibrium in the mind and body.

Breathing exercises help to increase the strength and efficiency of the respiratory system. In sports such as squash, tennis and badminton that demand much from the body in terms of strength, quick reflex action and flexibility, the practice of *pranayama* may be one of the most valuable yoga has to offer.

bridge pose, p.68

Easy yoga for dance and aerobics

Dance and aerobics both demand flexibility and strength. At first sight they may seem so similar to yoga that it is difficult to see why you might employ yoga as a method of cross-training. However, there are aspects of yoga that are quite unlike either dance or aerobics. The most important of these is the fact that poses can be held statically for long periods, either in an active phase, such as Boat pose, or in a passive phase such as Tailor pose (for both see opposite). Any statically held yoga pose might thus be of use in cross-training.

In Boat pose, strength is given to the abdominal area and back. This tunes the mind because it is a balance that needs to be held over a prolonged period. In Tailor pose the outward rotation of the legs is held in a relaxed way for a long time so the body gives in to gravitational pull and the inner thighs let go, producing deep and lasting stretch for hips and thighs. The balancing variation of Cat pose (below) helps to strengthen and tone the torso,

cat balancing variation, p. 84

making a stable centre for the body and improving core strength as well as providing a little easy work for the upper body in supporting the weight.

Dancers need to pay particular attention to keeping their breath slow and steady and on concentrating very fully on the feeling of the pose, rather than the way it looks. Minute and detailed observation of the sensations produced by each posture can be revealing, opening your awareness of a deeper level of body systems than bones and muscles alone.

boat pose, p.58

tailor pose, p.64

Bibliography

Coulter, H. D. and McCall, T. *Anatomy of Hatha Yoga: A Manual for Students, Teachers and Practitioners*, Body & Breath (Homedale, US), 2001

Desikachar, T. K. V. *The Heart of Yoga*, Inner Traditions International (New York), 1995

Fraser, T. *Yoga for You*, Duncan Baird (London) and Thorsons (New York), 2001

Fundamentals of Anatomy and Physiology, Prentice Hall (New Jersey, US), 2001

Harvey, P. *Yoga For Everybody – Simple Steps to a Strong Body and a Calm Mind*, Time Life (London and New York), 2001

Iyengar, B. K. S. *Light on Yoga*, Thorsons (London and New York), 1991

Iyengar, B. K. S. *Yoga: The Path to Holistic Health*, DK Publishing (London), 2001

Kogler, A. *Yoga for Athletes*, Llewellyn Publications (St Paul, US), 1999

Rawlinson, I. *Yoga for the West – a Manual for Designing Your Own Practice*, Unwin (London), 1988

Satyananda, S. *Asana Pranayama Mudra Bandha*, Bihar School of Yoga (Bihar, India), 1997

Satyananda, S. *Yoga Nidra*, Bihar School of Yoga (Bihar, India), 1998

Stiles, M. *Structural Yoga Therapy – Adapting to the Individual*, Samuel Weiser (York Beach, US), 2000

Wired Athletic Ability and the Anatomy of Motion, Mosby (St Louis, US), 1997

Index

Acknowledgments

My grateful thanks to Matthew Ward (photographer) for his consistent patience and good-humoured approach, which made shooting the photographs for this book a real pleasure. My husband Simon has contributed more toward this book than he could believe. Without his support, practical and emotional, this book would never have materialized at all. I also owe very special thanks to Tabitha Cowen who has kept me going with her boundless energy, enthusiasm and encouragement not just for this book, but generally for everything in life. A friend indeed!

Tara Fraser can be found at www.yogajunction.co.uk